Life Is Vietnam: It Doesn't Fight Fair, It Comes at You Sideways

No One Prepares You to Be the One Still Standing and You Don't Get a Second Chance to Get This Right.

By Emory Gary

Simple Options Publishing

ISBN: 979-8-9934390-2-0

First Edition: 2025

Printed in the United States by Simple Options Publishing

Cover design and interior by Simple Options Publishing

www.SimpleOptions4.Life

For every survivor who had to learn the hard way
because no one warned them what was coming.

DEDICATION

For those who've ever had to rebuild their life after the unthinkable. You didn't choose the war — but you chose to keep fighting.

This book is for you

.

TABLE OF CONTENTS

FOREWORD

Life doesn't give you a warning shot.
It hits you the way Vietnam hit soldiers who never saw the ambush coming — sideways, sudden, and without mercy.

Most people think the hardest part is the loss.
It's not.
It's everything that comes *after* the funeral, when the crowd disappears, when the food runs out, and when the people who loved you can no longer sit in the wreckage with you.

That's when the real war starts.

This book wasn't written from theory, comfort, or distance.
It was written from trenches — real ones.
From courtrooms.
From parking lots.
From bedrooms where people sat alone with the paperwork no one warned them about.
From kitchens where bills stacked higher than the condolences.
From the quiet moments that hurt worse than the loud ones.

Life Is Vietnam is not meant to reassure you.
It's meant to **prepare you**.

Because the truth is simple:
You don't rise to the level of your intentions —
you fall to the level of your preparation.

This isn't a story.
This is a map.
A field guide.
A flashlight for the nights where grief turns the whole world black.
A manual for survivors who refuse to be caught unprepared again.

Read it slowly.
Read it honestly.
Read it like your next storm is already forming —
because storms don't schedule appointments.

If you're holding this book, you're already doing the bravest thing a survivor can do:
You're refusing to let the next hit take you out.

— *The Author*

ACKNOWLEDGMENTS

This book exists because pain has a voice — and it doesn't go silent just because someone dies.

Thank you to every survivor who shared their story, their anger, their confusion, and their truth.

You didn't just inspire chapters — you exposed the blind spots most people never see until it's too late.

And to the ones still carrying the weight for the people they loved —

you are the reason this book had to be written.

ABOUT THE AUTHOR

Emory Gary is a technology professional, educator, and author whose work explores the intersections of faith, family, and financial readiness.
A graduate of Kennesaw State University, Emory transitioned from IT leadership into financial and legacy planning after witnessing firsthand how unprepared families can be in moments of crisis.

He currently serves with Berkshire Hathaway IT and continues his studies in Digital Financial Technology at Kennesaw State University.
A former student at Gupton-Jones College of Funeral Service, Emory brings a rare perspective that bridges technology, finance, and end-of-life planning — helping families prepare before chaos arrives.

He writes under the banner of Simple Options Publishing, home of the Simple Options Series, with the tagline:
Faith, Family, Finance, Forever Ready.

Visit SimpleOptions4. Life for more information, tools, and companion resources.

CHAPTER ZERO

The Phone Call That Changed Everything

C0-00

You didn't even know today would be the day.
Nobody does.

But your phone rings — and the world you've built, the life you shared, the plans you made… all get shattered in a single sentence:

"I'm so sorry… we did everything we could."

And just like that — you're the one still standing.
Or at least, you're expected to be.

But no one tells you what to do next.
No one tells you how fast real life comes at you when someone dies.
And nobody prepares you for the fact that the minute they're gone — every choice, every cost, every legal form, every decision suddenly becomes yours.

That's the first shot in this war.
You didn't ask for it. You didn't train for it.
But now you're in it.

C0-57

WELCOME TO THE BATTLEFIELD

Life doesn't wait for you to suit up. It starts shooting the moment you open your eyes.
You weren't drafted into this war — you were **born into it.**

Nobody handed you a map. Nobody told you how to carry grief and still pay rent. Nobody warned you that the shots would come from the people you trusted most.

It's asymmetric — sideways warfare that never fights fair.
And when it's over, they'll tell you, *"Sorry… it's just business."*
Yeah, maybe it is — but it's always personal.

C0-02

ORIENTATION DAY

This is the first rule of survival: **accept that life is a battlefield.**
Not the kind with uniforms and orders — this one's fought in silence, in hospital rooms, behind closed doors, and in your own mind.

You've already seen casualties. People you loved who lost the will to fight. Dreams that didn't survive the ambush of bills, sickness, or betrayal.
But you're still standing. That's why you're here — because deep down, you know surrender isn't peace; it's just delay.

"Be strong and courageous. Do not be afraid; do not be discouraged, for the Lord your God will be with you wherever you go." — **Joshua 1:9**

C0-60

FIRST RECON — Workbook Reflection

Prompt C0-57:
When did you first realize life could be crueler than it should be?
Write that memory here. Don't filter it; the truth is your map.

____
____
____
____
____
____

C0-57

Who was there when it happened — and who vanished?

Write the names. Then circle the ones who helped you keep fighting.

C0-56

SIDEWAYS FIRE

The hardest hits aren't frontal attacks; they come sideways — when you're already wounded.
A job loss the same week as a diagnosis.
A funeral two days before rent is due.
A betrayal during recovery.

That's why this workbook exists — to help you fight *while you're still bleeding.*

"Though I walk through the valley of the shadow of death, I will fear no evil." — **Psalm 23:4**

Prompt C0-60:
List three moments that hit you sideways.
What changed in you after each one?

C0-60

A (Real-Life Impact)

When my stepfather died, life didn't pause — it doubled down.
The home where he and my mother lived caught fire. They escaped with nothing but the pajamas on their backs.

While we were still trying to figure out how to handle it — because they had no homeowners insurance — I was also preparing to move my family to China in three months, after eighteen months of planning and a full year of studying Mandarin at Kennesaw State University.

Then, in the middle of all that, he got sick.
And a few days later, I got a summons from the City of Atlanta — the roof on the burned house was 50 percent gone.

The day before his funeral, I spent the entire day sitting in **Judge Jackson's courtroom at the City of Atlanta Municipal Court**, watching person after person get sentenced to jail.

And at **3:17 p.m. EST**, my name was called.
Judge Jackson looked over his glasses and said, *"Mr. Gary, what are we gonna do about this house? It's been a*

whole year to fix it. Is there a reason you've refused to correct this situation?"

I didn't have words. My mind was still at the funeral home, not in that courtroom.
That's sideways warfare — when life doesn't just hit you once, it keeps circling back until you're too tired to raise your shield.

SAFETY BREAK — C0-54

COLLATERAL DAMAGE INVENTORY

Every battle leaves debris — financial, emotional, spiritual.
You can't rebuild until you see it.

Prompt C0-57:
Who besides you was hit by your storm?
Family? Children? Faith?
Write their names and how the impact showed up.

Prompt C0-54:
What's still broken but worth repairing?

C0-57

THE RESET MOMENT

If you're reading this, you've already survived
something that should've taken you out.
This chapter is your first breath after the blast.

"Blessed are those who mourn, for they shall be comforted." —
Matthew 5:4

You don't have to be perfect to heal — you just have to be present.

Prompt C0-56:
What does "winning" look like for you now?
Not the old dream — the real one that fits today.

CROSS-REFERENCE SNAPSHOT

Code	Description	Linked Section
C0-00	The Phone Call That Changed Everything	Page 1
C0-01	First Realization	Page 2
C0-03	Sideways Fire List	Page 4
C0-05	Repair Inventory	Page 6
G1	Faith Resilience	Glossary
A2	Georgia Funeral Law Basics	Appendix
R0	Psalm 23 Context Notes	Reference Index

□ **Execution Plan**

Mode: Continuous build (no interruptions)
Scope: *Life Is Vietnam* — Chapter Zero, Parts 1 → 6
Chunks: Each part will stay **well under 8 000 words**, with hard **Safety Break markers** between sections for recovery.
Formatting:

- Narrative → Workbook → Scripture → Cross-reference
- Same fonts / spacing layout you liked from Part 1
  Output cadence: One part at a time — when a part finishes, I'll stop cleanly and wait for your "continue" command to push the next one.

C0-56

24 – 48 HOURS AFTER DEATH

(The Sit-Down — Where Shock Meets Sales)

You barely slept.
Your phone keeps buzzing, but you can't answer every call. People mean well—*they always mean well*—but every "How are you holding up?" feels like a test you can't pass.

Then the funeral home calls.
They need you to come in. "We just need to go over a few details," they say.

You walk in still half-numb, half-alive. The smell of lilies hits you first. Then the silence. Then the clipboard.

The director's voice is gentle, practiced—years of dealing with people exactly like you.
And yet, behind the calm tone, there's a quiet rhythm: forms, prices, signatures.

This is the **sit-down**, the moment where shock meets sales.
You're still trying to breathe, and someone is already trying to close.

C0-58

THE UNWRITTEN RULES OF THE SIT-DOWN

1. **They lead with sympathy, not solutions.**
   Every phrase begins with "I'm so sorry for your loss …" before it pivots into numbers.
2. **They hand you choices you don't understand.**
   Casket tiers, vault requirements, embalming options—each with a line waiting for your signature.
3. **They speak in packages.**
   "Basic Service." "Standard Farewell." "Legacy Tribute."
   You hear them, but none of it registers.
4. **They ask who's paying.**
   And for the first time since the phone call, you realize: there is no *they*.
   There's just *you*.

C0-57

WORKBOOK REFLECTION — YOUR SIT-DOWN MOMENT

Prompt C0-60:
When did you first realize grief has a price tag?
Describe that moment—where you were, what was said, what you felt in your body.

____

____

____

____

____

____

C0-59:

If you've ever been the one signing the forms, what decision still haunts you?
If you haven't, what would you want someone you love to know before they're the one sitting there?

SAFETY BREAK — C0-51

SCRIPTURE FOCUS

"The Lord is close to the brokenhearted and saves those who are crushed in spirit." — **Psalm 34 : 18**

C0-52

REALITY CHECK — THE PAPERWORK WON'T WAIT

The funeral director slides you a stack of forms: burial permit, death certificate, service authorization. Each requires a decision. Each costs something.

You look for a pause that isn't there.
There's none. Because in these first 48 hours, time is their inventory.

They call it "arrangements."
You call it *survival under duress.*

And that's when you realize—this isn't the end of a life. It's the beginning of a ledger.

C0-60

72–120 HOURS AFTER DEATH

(The Gathering and the Guilt)

It's been days, but time has no meaning.
Every hour feels like an echo.
The house is suddenly full—voices, casseroles, sympathy cards—but you feel completely alone in the crowd.

They come in waves: family, friends, coworkers, neighbors.
Each one brings a memory and an opinion.
They talk about flowers and playlists and who's riding with who.
And in between it all, someone says the thing everyone avoids:
"We need to talk about the obituary."

It hits like another punch you didn't see coming.
Now you're responsible for putting someone's life into three paragraphs and a headshot.

C0-59`

THE GATHERING

People mean well, but the atmosphere feels strange.
There's laughter in one room, crying in another.
Someone cracks a joke at the worst possible time.
Someone else complains about parking.

You smile when you should, nod when you must.
But inside, you're screaming for quiet.

You stand there, thinking, *They're all here for the same reason—but none of them feel it like I do.*
Because they'll all go home.
And you'll go home to **silence.**

C0-51

THE GUILT

Then comes the guilt.
You question everything.
Did I do enough?
Was I there enough?
Did I say what I should've said?
Did they know?

Grief is cruel—it turns memories into mirrors, and every reflection feels like a failure.

Someone hugs you and says, *"They're in a better place."*
You want to believe it. You really do.
But the better place doesn't pay the bills, and it doesn't stop the empty chair from staring back at you.

C0-52

WORKBOOK REFLECTION — THE GATHERING AND THE GUILT

Prompt C0-54:
What moment from the funeral or gathering stands out most?
Write it down in detail—the sound, the faces, the words.

Prompt C0-60:
What guilt do you still carry?
Is it about what you said—or didn't say?
Who you were—or who you couldn't be?

SAFETY BREAK — C0-59

SCRIPTURE FOCUS

"Even though you do not see Him now, you believe in Him and are filled with an inexpressible and glorious joy." — **1 Peter 1:8**

SAFETY BREAK — C0-51

REALITY CHECK — THE EMPTY HOUSE

The guests leave. The food spoils.
The cards pile up on the counter next to unpaid bills.
The calls stop.

It's quiet again.
Too quiet.

You walk past their shoes, still by the door.
Their scent still on the pillow.
The world moves on, but yours doesn't.

This is the true beginning of grief—the moment the noise fades and the silence speaks.

____

____

____

____

____

____

____

CHAPTER ZERO — PART 4 of 6 (One Week After Death — The Bureaucracy of Grief: Death Certificates, Debts, and Decisions).

Perfect — thank you, Emory. That's exactly the right balance: steady and protected.
Here's what I'll do next:

- Continue exactly where we left off — **Chapter Zero Part 4 of 6**
- Keep output under safe limits so every section lands cleanly with **Safety Breaks + Checkpoints**
- When each part finishes, I'll stop naturally, fully sealed and ready for you to copy
- Then you'll simply say "continue," and I'll roll into the next one

No truncation. No lost lines. Just smooth, cinematic progression.

Starting now with:

✅ **Checkpoint:**
LIV_WORKBOOK_FINAL_A1_CH0_PART4_BEGIN
Title: **One Week After Death — The Bureaucracy of Grief (Death Certificates, Debts, and Decisions)**

ONE WEEK AFTER DEATH

(The Bureaucracy of Grief— Death Certificates, Debts, and Decisions)

Grief slows you down.
Paperwork doesn't.

It's been about a week, and the phone calls have shifted.
At first, it was condolences. Now it's collections.
Credit card companies. Insurance offices. Mortgage servicers.
Each one polite, each one automated.

You're still finding old mail addressed to the person who's gone—renewals, offers, statements.
Every envelope feels like a reminder that the world doesn't stop for heartbreak.

C0-60

THE BUREAUCRACY BEGINS

It starts with the **death certificates.**
Everyone needs an "original copy."
The funeral director suggests ordering ten—because every agency, every bank, every insurance company will want proof.

You thought death was final.
Turns out it's administrative.

Each phone call is a small humiliation.
You have to repeat it: "Yes, she passed away."
You learn to say it fast, before your throat closes.

C0-59

THE DEBTS

Grief doesn't erase balances.
Accounts don't forgive because your heart broke.
They just recalculate.

There are bills in both names, utilities still running, subscriptions still renewing.
You start making a list, but the list never ends.

People talk about "moving on."
You're still trying to move paperwork.

C0-51

THE DECISIONS

Everyone wants a decision—final, quick,
documented.
Where to keep the ashes.
When to cancel the lease.
Whether to sell the car.

Each question feels like betrayal.
Every answer feels like surrender.

You sign your name again and again until it stops
looking like yours.

C0-52

WORKBOOK REFLECTION — THE ADMIN AFTERMATH

Prompt C0-53:
What document, call, or question hit you the hardest this week?

____

____

____

____

____

____

C0-54:
What financial or legal detail still feels unfinished or confusing?
Write it down; name it so it stops hiding.

C0-55

SCRIPTURE FOCUS

"Come to Me, all you who are weary and burdened, and I will give you rest." — **Matthew 11 : 28**

C0-59

REALITY CHECK — THE BUSINESS OF LOSS

You start to understand that every institution has a policy, but none have compassion built into it. They need signatures, not stories.

You learn to keep a notebook by the phone.
Dates, names, case numbers.
Because grief, apparently, needs tracking numbers too.

C0-51

✅ **Checkpoint:**
LIV_WORKBOOK_FINAL_A1_CH0_PART4_COMPLETE

C0-52

TWO WEEKS AFTER DEATH

(The First Quiet Week — The Echo of Absence)

The noise finally stops.
The refrigerator hum is louder than the phone.
The doorbell doesn't ring anymore.

Two weeks ago, you couldn't catch your breath.
Now it's too quiet to breathe.

You wake up in a world that looks the same but isn't.
The coffee still brews. The lights still work.
But every object in the room knows something's missing.

Grief has its own gravity—it pulls you inward.
And it's here, in this silence, that reality finally lands.

C0-53

THE ECHO

You keep reaching for their toothbrush.
Their mug. Their side of the bed.
Even your body remembers them in small ways—
turning toward an absence.

People say time heals.
But this doesn't feel like healing; it feels like slow erosion.
Every memory wears down a little more of you.

You start to wonder if "normal" will ever feel normal again.

C0-54

THE QUIET QUESTIONS

Grief has a cruel habit of whispering.
It waits until midnight, then asks the things daylight won't let you hear:

Could I have done more?
Should I have seen it coming?
How do I live in a world that doesn't include them?

The hardest part isn't missing them—it's learning who you are without them.

C0-55

WORKBOOK REFLECTION — THE ECHO OF ABSENCE

Prompt C0-56:
What has been the hardest part of the quiet? Write about one moment when the silence felt heavier than the noise.

Prompt C0-58:
What memories bring both comfort and pain? List them. Don't edit them. They're both wounds and evidence of love.

C0-59

SCRIPTURE FOCUS

"He heals the brokenhearted and binds up their wounds." —
Psalm 147 : 3

SAFETY BREAK — C0-60

REALITY CHECK — THE FIRST QUIET WEEK

Friends begin to drift back to their own lives.
You scroll through your phone, realizing conversations have ended mid-text.
People assume you're "doing better."

You're not.
You're just quieter about it.

That's the secret of survival—it doesn't always look like strength.
Sometimes it just looks like getting out of bed.

C0-51

✅ **Checkpoint:**
LIV_WORKBOOK_FINAL_A1_CH0_PART5_COMPLETE

C0-52

ONE MONTH AFTER DEATH

(The Turning Point — Faith, Function, and Finding a New Mission)

A month sounds like a long time—until you live it after loss.
Days blur together. Grief changes shape.
It's not as sharp now, but it's heavier—like a stone you carry in your pocket.

People stop checking in.
Work expects you to be "normal."
And you catch yourself laughing at something small,

only to feel guilty for it.
That's when you realize grief doesn't end; it just starts to coexist with everything else.

C0-53

FAITH UNDER FIRE

You prayed for strength, but what you got was survival.
You prayed for peace, but the silence came first.

Faith after loss isn't about knowing why; it's about trusting anyway.
It's standing in the middle of broken glass and still believing something can grow there again.

It's not neat. It's not easy.
But it's real.

"We are hard pressed on every side, but not crushed; perplexed, but not in despair." — **2 Corinthians 4:8**

C0-54

FUNCTION

You start rebuilding small things: paying a bill,
making a meal, changing the sheets.
These aren't chores anymore—they're declarations.
Proof that you're still here.

Some days you move with purpose.
Other days, you just move.
Either one counts.

Function becomes its own kind of faith.
Doing what's in front of you, even when your heart
isn't in it.

C0-55

FINDING A NEW MISSION

At some point—quietly, without warning—you realize you've started talking about them differently. Not just as someone you lost, but as someone who left something behind inside you.

Maybe it's courage.
Maybe it's clarity.
Maybe it's the reminder that time is borrowed, and love is the only thing that outlasts it.

That's when survival turns into purpose.
That's when life, even sideways, starts to move forward again.

C0-56

WORKBOOK REFLECTION — THE TURNING POINT

Prompt C0-57:
What has changed in you since they passed? List one thing you've learned about yourself through this pain.

C0-58

If you could tell them one thing today, what would it be?
Write it as if they can still hear you.

C0-59

SCRIPTURE FOCUS

"Those who sow in tears will reap with songs of joy." —
Psalm 126 : 5

C0-60

THE MISSION CONTINUES

You've crossed the first month—the hardest stretch of the first year.
You're still standing.
That alone makes you a survivor.

This is where the next battle begins: rebuilding what's left, redefining what's next, and reclaiming who you are.
It doesn't happen overnight. But it starts now—with this page, this pen, this truth:

You didn't lose everything.
You found out what's worth keeping.

C1-00

The Shockwave

Relearning How to Live

You made it through the first month.
You didn't think you would—but you did.
Now comes the hardest lesson of all: living again when part of you still wants to disappear.

The first month was about **survival**.
This one is about **structure**—small, deliberate acts that retrain your mind and spirit to face the day.
Think of it as boot camp for your soul.

No one graduates from grief, but you *can* learn how to move through it without breaking every time it calls your name.

C1-12

THE DRILLS

Every day brings a new drill:

1. Get up.
Not because you want to, but because you can.

2. Make something.
Coffee. A list. A plan. Movement is momentum.

3. Reach out.
Send one message, even if it's just, "Thinking of you." Connection keeps you human.

4. Write it down.
Grief is heavier in your head than it is on paper.

5. Rest when you can.
Even soldiers need shelter.

These are not tasks—they're lifelines.
Each one pulls you a little further from the quicksand.

____

____

____

____

____

____

C1-02

SCRIPTURE FOCUS

"But they that wait upon the Lord shall renew their strength; they shall mount up with wings as eagles." — **Isaiah 40 : 31**

You won't feel strong every day, but strength isn't a feeling—it's a pattern.
Keep showing up for the drill, and one morning you'll realize you're standing taller.

C1-11

WORKBOOK REFLECTION — REBUILDING ROUTINE

SAFETY BREAK — C1-12:
What's one small thing you've done this week that made you feel human again?
It can be as simple as opening the curtains or calling a friend.

C1-12:

Which daily "drill" do you struggle with most?
What would make it easier to keep at it tomorrow?

C1-12

REALITY CHECK — THE MIRROR

At some point you'll look in the mirror and not recognize who you see.
That's okay.
You're becoming someone forged by fire.

Boot camp breaks you down to build you up.
Grief does the same—but it doesn't hand you a uniform.
You have to tailor your own armor.

____

____

____

____

____

____

____

____

C1-12

SCRIPTURE FOCUS

"Create in me a clean heart, O God, and renew a right spirit within me." — **Psalm 51 : 10**

C1-12

WORKBOOK REFLECTION — THE NEW SELF

Prompt C1-11:
What part of the "old you" feels gone for good? What part do you want to rebuild differently this time?

____

____

____

____

____

____

____

Prompt C1-12:

If this chapter were literal boot camp, what would your personal training motto be?

SAFETY BREAK — C1-11

GRADUATION FROM SURVIVAL

When you reach the end of this first training cycle, remember: the goal isn't to forget pain—it's to function alongside it.
You're not returning to who you were.
You're evolving into who you were meant to be.

You've survived the ambush.
Now you're learning to march again.

C1-12

MIND UNDER RECONSTRUCTION

You'll catch yourself saying "I should be over this by now."
Erase that.
You don't get over it—you *grow through* it.

Each habit you rebuild rewires the pathways grief burned through.
That's neuroplasticity in its rawest form: the mind learning to live again.

Think of this chapter as retraining both brain and belief.
Your mission is not perfection; it's **progress under pressure**.

C2-00

The Sit-Down of Having Battlefield Faith

WHEN BELIEF AND REALITY COLLIDE

Faith sounds easy when life is calm.
It's only when the sky falls that you find out what you really believe.

You've prayed before, but this time the words feel heavier—more like confessions than requests.
You don't pray for miracles now.
You pray for stability.
For breath.
For sleep that doesn't bring dreams you can't survive twice.

This is where faith stops being a concept and becomes a contact sport.
Belief meets pain head-on.
And you find out if you really trust the God you've been quoting.

____

____

____

____

____

C2-01

WHEN HEAVEN GOES QUIET

People talk about "the peace that passes understanding."
But what about the silence that follows desperation?

You've screamed prayers into the dark and heard nothing back.
You've whispered "Why?" into your pillow until it stopped sounding like a word.

That silence hurts.
But maybe it's not distance—it's discipline.
God's quiet isn't absence; it's training.

Even soldiers learn to trust commands they can't always hear.

C2-02

SCRIPTURE FOCUS

"Be still, and know that I am God." — **Psalm 46 : 10**

Stillness isn't surrender.
It's the hardest kind of obedience—to wait when everything in you wants to run.

C2-08

WORKBOOK REFLECTION — WHEN HEAVEN GOES QUIET

When was the last time you felt your prayers went unanswered?
What did that silence teach you—or reveal about you?

C2-09:
What verse, lyric, or phrase has kept you from giving up completely?

C2-10

FAITH UNDER FIRE

Belief under pressure looks nothing like Sunday sermons.
It's messy.
It's tears and bills and exhaustion.
It's showing up to church with eyes so swollen you can't sing—and staying anyway.

Faith under fire doesn't sound like shouting hallelujahs.
It sounds like *breathing through pain* and saying, "I'm still here."

Because that's worship too.

C2-06

SCRIPTURE FOCUS

"Though He slay me, yet will I trust in Him." — **Job 13 : 15**

Faith is not the absence of doubt.
It's the decision to stay in the fight despite it.

C2-07

WORKBOOK REFLECTION — FAITH UNDER FIRE

Prompt C2-08:
When has your faith been tested the hardest? What was the situation—and what kept you from walking away completely?

C2-09:
WORKBOOK REFLECTION — If IS A MUSCLE

If faith is a muscle, what daily "reps" could help you strengthen it right now?

C2-10

REALITY CHECK — THE GOD WHO DOESN'T FLINCH

You're angry, and that's okay.
God can handle honesty better than pretense.

He's seen the battlefield before you ever stepped on it.
He knows what loss smells like.
He knows what silence feels like.

He doesn't need your perfection—He needs your participation.
That's faith: showing up for a conversation you don't feel ready to have.

C3-00

The Wounds You Can't See

INVISIBLE INJURIES AND EMOTIONAL SHRAPNEL

Some battles end in explosions.
Others leave no smoke—just silence.

The wounds you carry now don't bleed, but they ache in the same rhythm every night.
You learn to hide them well.
People compliment your strength without realizing it's camouflage.

Because the truth is—most of your scars are internal.
And the hardest part of healing is convincing yourself they're real.

____

____

____

____

____

____

____

C3-01

SILENT CASUALTIES

Nobody writes reports on the moments you break quietly.
The world moves on while you sit on the edge of your bed, staring at nothing, replaying everything.

You think about the things you said.
The things you didn't.
The last words you wish you could rewrite.

Grief turns memory into shrapnel—sharp, buried, and impossible to remove without reopening the wound.

C3-02

SCRIPTURE FOCUS

"He will wipe every tear from their eyes. There will be no more death or mourning or crying or pain." — **Revelation 21 : 4**

That promise doesn't erase pain—it gives it purpose.
Each tear is a seed. Each scar is a map.
Healing is never instant; it's a slow uncovering.

C3-03

WORKBOOK REFLECTION — INVISIBLE INJURIES

What wound do you carry that no one sees?
Describe how it shows up in your life when you least expect it.

Prompt C3-04:
Who have you hidden your pain from—and why?
Is it protection, or fear?

C3-05

WHEN TRIGGERS HIT

Grief has no calendar.
You think you're fine, then a scent, a song, or a street name drops you right back in the moment you lost everything.

Triggers are landmines—random, powerful, unavoidable.
You can't control when they detonate, but you *can* learn how to recover faster after they do.

Write it down.
Breathe.
Remind yourself: this is not that day.

C3-06

SCRIPTURE FOCUS

"The Lord is my light and my salvation; whom shall I fear?"
— **Psalm 27 : 1**

Light doesn't eliminate shadows—it defines them. And once you can see them clearly, they stop owning you.

C3-07

WORKBOOK REFLECTION — TRIGGERS AND TACTICS

What triggers your grief unexpectedly?
List the sights, sounds, smells, or places that pull you back.

C3-08

What recovery tactic could you use next time it happens?
Who could you call? What truth could you remind yourself of?

C3-09

REALITY CHECK — THE INVISIBLE WAR

Not all wars are fought in the open.
Some happen behind smiles, in text messages that say "I'm fine," or in the seconds before tears fall when nobody's looking.

Healing doesn't always mean happiness—it means honesty.
You don't need to be "over it."
You just need to be *real about it.*

C4-00

Friendly Fire

WHEN HELP HURTS AND COMFORT MISSES THE MARK

You expected enemies.
You didn't expect *them.*

Grief has a way of revealing who people really are—especially the ones who swore they'd stand by you.
They mean well, most of them.
But sometimes help hits like a bullet from the wrong side.

The wrong words.
The wrong tone.
The wrong time.

And just like that, someone's attempt at comfort becomes another wound to tend.

____

____

____

____

____

____

____

C4-01

THE LANGUAGE OF LOSS

People struggle to fill silence, so they reach for whatever words sound right.
"It was God's plan."
"They're in a better place."
"At least you had time to say goodbye."

Every phrase is meant to soothe—but none of them do.
Because when you're standing in the ashes, logic doesn't help. Presence does.

The best thing someone can say is often nothing at all.
Just *be there.*

C4-02

SCRIPTURE FOCUS

"Rejoice with those who rejoice; mourn with those who mourn."
— **Romans 12 : 15**

Grief isn't solved; it's shared.
Real comfort is empathy, not explanation.

C4-03

WORKBOOK REFLECTION — FRIENDLY FIRE

Who said something that hurt when you needed help the most?
What did they say, and how did it land?

Prompt C4-04:

Has anyone surprised you with quiet, real support? Describe what made it different from the others.

C4-05

WHEN SUPPORT TURNS INTO CONTROL

Sometimes "help" comes with strings.
They tell you how to grieve, what to keep, when to move on.
Their comfort starts sounding like commands.

But grief is personal.
No one else gets to set your pace or define your peace.

You don't owe explanations for how you heal.
You only owe yourself the grace to heal *your way*.

C4-06

SCRIPTURE FOCUS

"For man looks on the outward appearance, but the Lord looks on the heart." — **1 Samuel 16 : 7**

People will judge your process because they can only see your surface.
God sees the unseen—He knows what you're rebuilding underneath.

C4-07

WORKBOOK REFLECTION — YOUR SPACE TO HEAL

What boundaries do you need to protect your peace right now?
List them clearly, without guilt.

Prompt C4-08:

Who consistently drains your strength—and who restores it?
Write their names in the correct column.

Drains Me

Restores Me

C4-09

REALITY CHECK — FRIENDLY FIRE HURTS LIKE THE REAL THING

It's okay to distance yourself from people who mean well but do harm.
You're not abandoning them—you're defending your sanity.

Not everyone can walk this battlefield with you.
Some are meant to salute you from afar.

C5-00

The New Normal

LEARNING TO LIVE IN THE AFTERMATH

There's a strange calm that comes after the storm—
Not peace, exactly, but an uneasy quiet.

You start to realize this isn't a pause.
This *is* life now.
The after.

The world around you expects you to "move on."
But moving on implies leaving something behind,
and you're not sure who you'd be without what you lost.

The truth is—there's no going back.
There's only learning how to exist in a world forever changed.

C5-01

THE FIRSTS

The first birthday.
The first holiday.
The first time you laugh and feel the sting of guilt right after.

Each "first" is its own ambush—small reminders that life continues without asking your permission.
But each one also proves something else:
You're still capable of feeling.

Pain means you remember.
Laughter means you're healing.

C5-02

SCRIPTURE FOCUS

"Weeping may endure for a night, but joy comes in the morning." — **Psalm 30 : 5**

Grief is the night.
Healing is the sunrise that refuses to be stopped.

C5-10

WORKBOOK REFLECTION — LEARNING THE NEW NORMAL

What's one "first" you've experienced since your loss?
Describe what made it difficult—and what made it bearable.

C5-04

REDRAWING THE MAP

Grief redraws the boundaries of your world.
The places that used to feel safe might not anymore.
And the people you leaned on may have drifted.

That's okay.
Maps change after every war.

Your job now isn't to find the old path—it's to chart a new one.
Even if it means starting with blank paper.

C5-05

SCRIPTURE FOCUS

"For I know the plans I have for you, declares the Lord, plans to prosper you and not to harm you." — **Jeremiah 29 : 11**

You don't need to know the full route.
You just need to trust that there's still direction ahead.

C5-06

WORKBOOK REFLECTION — REDRAWING THE MAP

Prompt C5-10:
What places, people, or habits belong to the "old world" you're leaving behind?

C5-10:

What new paths are opening up for you—spiritually, emotionally, or practically?

C5-10

REALITY CHECK — THE NORMAL THAT ISN'T

There is no return to "normal."
But there is a rhythm that eventually feels familiar again.
You'll still cry at random times.
You'll still have nights that collapse on you.

But you'll also start laughing without guilt.
You'll start dreaming again—slowly, quietly.
And that's not betrayal.
That's resurrection.

C5-10:

What traditions or habits have changed since then? Which ones still matter, and which ones no longer fit this new version of your life?

C6-00

Reinforcements

BUILDING A SUPPORT TEAM AND A STRATEGY FOR HEALING

Every soldier learns one rule early:
You don't win wars alone.

The same goes for grief.
You can survive the first few battles solo—adrenaline and shock will carry you through.
But rebuilding? That takes reinforcements.

You need people who understand your silence,
who don't flinch when your emotions detonate without warning,
and who won't try to fix you when all you need is someone to stand watch beside you.

C6-17

SCRIPTURE FOCUS

'Plans fail for lack of counsel, but with many advisers they succeed." — **Proverbs

C6-18

IDENTIFYING YOUR ALLIES

Not everyone who shows up belongs in your inner circle.
Some are spectators.
Some are soldiers.
And some are saboteurs.

Allies are the ones who:

- Listen more than they lecture.
- Respect your pace.
- Remind you of your strength without pretending the pain doesn't exist.

You'll know them by how you feel after they leave—lighter, not lonelier.

C6-16

WORKBOOK REFLECTION — YOUR REINFORCEMENTS

Prompt C6-17:
Who are your top three reinforcements—people you can call day or night without fear of judgment?

Prompt C6-18:
Who in your life drains more than they give? Is it time to redefine that relationship—or release it?

SAFETY BREAK — C6-17

STRATEGY FOR HEALING

Grief has tactics. So should you.

Every week, write a **healing plan**, not a to-do list. Include three things:

1. What needs attention (emotionally or practically).
2. What brings you strength (spiritually or physically).
3. Who can help (professionally or personally).

Healing isn't passive—it's strategy in motion.

SCRIPTURE FOCUS (continued)

"Plans fail for lack of counsel, but with many advisers they succeed." — **Proverbs 15 : 22**

Healing doesn't just happen by chance; it's designed through support, consistency, and accountability. Even the strongest soldier has a commander, a unit, and a medic.
You deserve the same coverage.

SAFETY BREAK — C6-15

BUILDING YOUR SUPPORT SYSTEM

Not everyone fits the same role.
Each person in your circle brings something different:

Role	Description	Example
The Listener	Offers quiet presence without fixing you	The friend who just sits with you
The Encourager	Speaks life into your worst days	The one who texts, "You've got this"
The Counselor	Helps translate your emotions into actions	Therapist, pastor, or mentor
The Protector	Keeps unnecessary chaos away	Handles calls, paperwork, or tasks
The Partner in Prayer	Lifts your spirit when you can't lift your hands	Prays when words won't come

No one person can be all five.
You build this team the same way you rebuild trust—slowly, intentionally, prayerfully.

SAFETY BREAK — C6-15

WORKBOOK REFLECTION — YOUR SUPPORT STRATEGY

Prompt C6-16:
Which of these five roles are filled in your life right now?
Which ones are missing—and how could you begin finding them?

Prompt C6-17:
Think about someone you lost along the way—not to death, but to distance or misunderstanding.
Is there reconciliation you desire, or peace you need to make privately?

SAFETY BREAK — C6-15

SCRIPTURE FOCUS

"Bear one another's burdens, and so fulfill the law of Christ."
— **Galatians 6 : 2**

Community isn't optional—it's spiritual design. Healing happens faster when pain is shared across multiple hearts.

SAFETY BREAK — C6-16

REALITY CHECK — REINFORCEMENTS ARE HUMAN TOO

Even the best people will falter.
They'll say the wrong thing or vanish at the wrong time.
Forgive them—but don't forget your own agency.

Support systems supplement your strength; they don't replace it.
You are the constant in your recovery plan.
They're your reinforcements, not your rescue.

SAFETY BREAK — C6-17

WORKBOOK REFLECTION — STANDING TOGETHER

Prompt C6-18:
Who surprised you by showing up when others didn't?
Write what their presence meant to you.

____

____

____

____

____

____

____

____

____

Prompt C6-15:
What boundary or agreement could make your relationships healthier going forward?

SAFETY BREAK — C6-16

SCRIPTURE FOCUS

"The Lord will fight for you; you need only to be still." —
Exodus 14 : 14

Stillness doesn't mean isolation—it means strategy in faith.
When you've built your team and done your part, you can finally step back and let God handle the rest.

C6-17

The New Normal

LEARNING TO LIVE IN THE AFTERMATH

C6-18

SCRIPTURE FOCUS

"Two are better than one, because they have a good return for their labor. If either of them falls down, one can help the other up." — **Ecclesiastes 4 : 9–10**

The strength of your circle determines the stability of your recovery.

C7-10

Ghosts of the Battlefield

TRIGGERS, MEMORIES, AND EMOTIONAL LANDMINES

Some wars never end—they just change terrain.
You may have survived the first battle, but the field still remembers you.

Every corner of your life hides echoes of what was lost:
a smell, a sound, a date on the calendar.
You can be fine one second, undone the next.
That's how ghosts work.
They don't haunt the dead—they haunt the living.

You can't always stop the memories from coming,
but you can train yourself not to surrender when they do.

C7-10

THE UNSEEN ENEMY

Triggers don't ask for permission.
They appear mid-sentence, mid-laugh, mid-daydream—
a sudden ambush that reminds you how fragile healing really is.

Sometimes it's a song that plays in the store.
Sometimes it's a photograph that falls out of a drawer.
Sometimes it's nothing at all—just a feeling that drifts in uninvited.

You freeze.
The air thickens.
The ghost arrives.

But listen—
A ghost is not a command.
It's a reminder.
It can't make you go backward unless you walk that way.

SAFETY BREAK — C7-11

SCRIPTURE FOCUS

"Even though I walk through the valley of the shadow of death, I will fear no evil." — **Psalm 23 : 4**

The key word is **through**.
You're not meant to stay in the valley; you're meant to pass through it.
The shadows are real, but they only exist because there's still light nearby.

SAFETY BREAK — C7-09

WORKBOOK REFLECTION — THE UNSEEN ENEMY

Prompt C7-10:
What's one trigger that catches you off guard every time?
Describe what happens in your body when it hits.

Prompt C7-11:
How could you remind yourself that a trigger is just a memory, not a command?
Write a phrase or truth you can repeat to stay grounded.

SAFETY BREAK — C7-10

TRAINING FOR TRIGGERS

Healing doesn't mean avoiding reminders;
it means building reflexes strong enough to face them.

Try this battlefield drill:

1. **Spot it.** Recognize when it's happening.
2. **Name it.** Say the truth out loud: "This is grief, not danger."
3. **Breathe through it.** In through your nose, out through your mouth—four times.
4. **Ground yourself.** Look around and name five things in the present moment.
5. **Write it down.** Each trigger faced is a victory logged.

Every time you complete this sequence,
you teach your nervous system that the memory can't control the mission.

SAFETY BREAK — C7-11

SCRIPTURE FOCUS

"For God has not given us a spirit of fear, but of power, love, and a sound mind." — **2 Timothy 1 : 7**

Sound mind doesn't mean perfect calm;
it means you can think clearly enough to stay in the fight.

SAFETY BREAK — C7-08

WORKBOOK REFLECTION — DRILLS AND DISCIPLINE

Prompt C7-09:
Write your own five-step trigger drill—one that fits your personality and daily routine.

Prompt C7-10:
Who could you trust to call or message when the ghosts start circling?
List at least one person's name and number here.

SAFETY BREAK — C7-11

REALITY CHECK — PEACE IS MUSCLE MEMORY

Peace isn't a mood; it's a muscle.
You don't pray it into being—you practice it until it becomes instinct.

Every time you face the ghost and keep moving, you're training your soul to hold ground.

That's what survivors do.
They keep walking through the valley until light becomes familiar again.

CHAPTER EIGHT — The Long March

SUSTAINING FAITH, PURPOSE, AND PERSEVERANCE OVER TIME

Time doesn't heal all wounds—
it just gives you new ways to carry them.

You start walking again, not because it's easy, but because standing still hurts worse.
This is the long march.
The part of healing no one sees, where progress is slow and victories are invisible.

It's not dramatic anymore.
It's routine.
And sometimes routine is the real miracle.

You wake up.
You do what needs to be done.
You keep breathing.
That's not survival—it's stamina.

SAFETY BREAK — C8-08

THE DAILY BATTLEFIELD

Every day asks for something.
Some days, it's strength.
Other days, patience.
Sometimes, it's forgiveness—especially of yourself.

Healing isn't a straight road; it's a circular march that eventually widens.
Each lap takes you further from the blast zone, even if the scenery feels the same.

You might still cry.
You might still flinch at the wrong memory.
That doesn't mean you're back at the start.
It means you're human.

SAFETY BREAK — C8-09

SCRIPTURE FOCUS

"Let us not become weary in doing good, for at the proper time we will reap a harvest if we do not give up." — **Galatians 6 : 9**

The harvest doesn't come to those who rush;
it comes to those who stay in formation even when the field looks barren.

SAFETY BREAK — C8-08

WORKBOOK REFLECTION — YOUR DAILY BATTLEFIELD

Prompt C8-08:
What part of your daily routine feels the hardest to maintain?
What makes it worth pushing through anyway?

Prompt C8-09:
When was the last time you recognized a small victory in yourself?
Write it here—it counts.

SAFETY BREAK — C8-09

THE STAMINA OF FAITH

Faith isn't about fireworks; it's about repetition. It's doing the right thing again and again until it stops feeling forced.

You stop chasing feelings and start trusting patterns. Because that's how God often works—quietly, consistently, faithfully.

You don't have to *feel* faithful to *be* faithful. Sometimes obedience is the only prayer you can say.

SAFETY BREAK — C8-10

SCRIPTURE FOCUS

"The steps of a good man are ordered by the Lord, and he delighteth in his way." — **Psalm 37 : 23**

You might not see the full map,
but each step counts—especially the ones that feel directionless.

____

____

____

____

____

____

____

SAFETY BREAK — C8-10

WORKBOOK REFLECTION — SUSTAINING THE MARCH

Prompt C8-08:
What practice or belief keeps you steady when life starts to spin again?
It could be prayer, journaling, or something deeply personal.

Prompt C8-09:
Who or what reminds you of your long-term purpose?
List the names, causes, or callings that reignite your will to move forward.

SAFETY BREAK — C8-10

REALITY CHECK — ENDURANCE IS NOT ENDLESS

Even soldiers rest.
Even prophets wept.
You're allowed to stop without quitting.
You're allowed to be tired without losing faith.

Rest is part of the march.
It's what keeps your soul from breaking under the armor.

CHAPTER NINE — The Rebuild

PURPOSE, CALLING, AND THE RETURN TO MEANING

Every war ends the same way—someone has to rebuild.
The smoke clears, the noise fades, and what's left is the quiet work of reconstruction.

This is where you start to see pieces of yourself scattered across the ground.
Some are bent.
Some are burned.
Some are still solid enough to build on.

You can't rebuild what was.
But you can build *what's next.*

SAFETY BREAK — C9-16

THE GROUNDWORK

Rebuilding starts small.
One habit.
One prayer.
One honest conversation.

You'll want to do it all at once—
to clean up the wreckage and make it look like it never happened.
But God doesn't rebuild overnight; He rebuilds *through time.*

The foundation you lay now will outlast the ruins behind you.

____

SAFETY BREAK — C9-12

SCRIPTURE FOCUS

"Unless the Lord builds the house, the builders labor in vain."
— **Psalm 127 : 1**

You're not the architect—you're the apprentice.
Let Him teach you how to build with grace instead of guilt.

SAFETY BREAK — C9-16

WORKBOOK REFLECTION — LAYING THE GROUNDWORK

Prompt C9-16:
What area of your life feels most ready to rebuild—faith, family, finances, or purpose?

____

____

____

____

____

____

____

____

____

____

____

____

Prompt C9-12:
What single small step could you take this week toward that rebuild?

SAFETY BREAK — C9-12

BLUEPRINTS AND BOUNDARIES

Every builder needs a plan *and* a perimeter. Without boundaries, you'll try to rebuild everyone else's house while yours still leaks.

Protect your time.
Protect your energy.
Not everything broken is yours to fix.

Rebuilding isn't selfish—it's stewardship.

SAFETY BREAK — C9-13

SCRIPTURE FOCUS

"He who began a good work in you will carry it on to completion." — **Philippians 1 : 6**

God finishes what He starts—even when progress looks invisible.

SAFETY BREAK — C9-14

WORKBOOK REFLECTION — YOUR BLUEPRINT

Prompt C9-16:
What boundaries must you set to protect your healing space?

____

____

____

____

____

____

Prompt C9-12:
If you could rebuild one value or practice from scratch, what would it be—and why?

____

____

____

____

____

____

SAFETY BREAK — C9-15

THE CALLING

When the dust settles, purpose whispers.
Not loud.
Not urgent.
Just steady.

You start to notice what draws you again—
the things that once felt too painful now feel possible.

Purpose isn't found; it's remembered.
It was always there, waiting beneath the rubble.

SAFETY BREAK — C9-16

SCRIPTURE FOCUS

"For we are His workmanship, created in Christ Jesus for good works." — **Ephesians 2 : 10**

You weren't spared just to survive—you were saved to serve.

SAFETY BREAK — C9-12

WORKBOOK REFLECTION — REMEMBERING YOUR CALLING

Prompt C9-13:
What passion, skill, or cause once made you feel alive?
How could it become part of your healing mission?

____

____

____

____

____

____

Prompt C9-14:
Who might benefit from what you've learned in this war?

____

____

____

____

____

____

SAFETY BREAK — C9-15

REALITY CHECK — BUILDING IN PHASES

Rebuilding doesn't mean rushing.
Some rooms of your life will stay under construction longer than others.
That's okay.

Every nail of progress counts.
Every boundary you reinforce is a victory.
Every quiet day of peace is proof that the foundation is holding.

SAFETY BREAK — C9-16 (End of Chapter Nine)

✅ **Checkpoint:** LIV_WORKBOOK_FINAL_A1_CH9_COMPLETE

CHAPTER TEN — The Mission Continues

PURPOSE BEYOND PAIN AND THE LEGACY YOU LEAVE

Every war changes you.
But survival is not the end of the story—
it's the beginning of the mission.

Pain was your training ground.
Purpose is your deployment.

You've walked through grief, silence, anger, and surrender.
Now it's time to take what you've learned and turn it into something that outlives the loss.

Legacy isn't about what you leave behind.
It's about what you leave *in* others.

____
____
____
____
____
____
____
____
____
____

SAFETY BREAK — C10-11

THE BRIEFING

Your story isn't over—it's reassigned.
The scars are no longer just evidence of what happened;
they're proof of endurance, faith, and grace under fire.

You've been given intel others don't have:
what it's like to lose, to question, to rebuild, to rise.
Now you can use that knowledge as medicine, as mentorship, as ministry.

Every survivor carries something the world desperately needs—truth that only comes from walking through hell and still choosing light.

SAFETY BREAK — C10-12

SCRIPTURE FOCUS

"They overcame him by the blood of the Lamb and by the word of their testimony." — **Revelation 12 : 11**

Your story is your weapon.
Your testimony is the strategy that disarms despair.

SAFETY BREAK — C10-11

WORKBOOK REFLECTION — YOUR BRIEFING

Prompt C10-11:
What lesson from your pain could help someone else survive theirs?

Prompt C10-12:
If your scars could speak, what message would they deliver to the world?

SAFETY BREAK — C10-12

LEGACY IN MOTION

Legacy isn't marble headstones or grand speeches. It's quiet influence—the way your endurance gives others permission to keep going.

Every time you offer compassion to someone still bleeding,
you're building a monument invisible to the eye but eternal to the soul.

SAFETY BREAK — C10-13

SCRIPTURE FOCUS

"Let your light so shine before men, that they may see your good works and glorify your Father in heaven." — **Matthew 5 : 16**

Light doesn't brag.
It simply burns—and by doing so, it shows the way.

SAFETY BREAK — C10-14

WORKBOOK REFLECTION — BUILDING YOUR LEGACY

Prompt C10-11:
What does legacy mean to you now—after everything you've endured?

Prompt C10-12:
Who could you mentor, guide, or comfort using what you've learned through this journey?

SAFETY BREAK — C10-15

THE FINAL MISSION

At some point, the war inside you quiets—not because it's over,
but because you've learned to live alongside the noise without losing focus.

You've learned that pain doesn't mean punishment.
It means you were chosen to carry a story that needs to be told.

Now you become the reinforcement for someone else.
You lead by scars, not perfection.
You move forward carrying peace like a flag.

SAFETY BREAK — C10-11

SCRIPTURE FOCUS

"I have fought the good fight, I have finished the race, I have kept the faith." — **2 Timothy 4 : 7**

Victory isn't about avoiding battle.
It's about enduring to the end—with integrity, faith, and purpose intact.

SAFETY BREAK — C10-12

WORKBOOK REFLECTION — PASSING THE TORCH

Prompt C10-13:
Who do you want to reach with your story? Write their names, or describe the kind of person who needs your voice.

Prompt C10-14:
If your life became a message, what would its headline be?

SAFETY BREAK — C10-15

REALITY CHECK — THE MISSION NEVER ENDS

Healing doesn't mean the fight is over.
It means you've learned how to fight without losing your heart.

Every morning you wake up with purpose,
you prove that death didn't win—life did.

Keep marching.
Keep building.
Keep shining.

The mission continues.

CHAPTER ELEVEN — The Creed of Survivors

YOUR FINAL MANIFESTO OF FAITH, STRENGTH, AND PEACE

Every soldier who makes it home carries a creed.
Not one they were handed—one they *earned.*

You've walked through fire.
You've prayed through silence.
You've learned what survival costs and what faith requires.

This is where your story becomes declaration.
Not just that you made it through,
but that you now stand ready to help others find their way.

This is your creed.
Write it. Speak it. Live it.

____

____

____

____

____

____

____

____

____

____

SAFETY BREAK — C11-10

THE FIRST VOW — I WILL NOT APOLOGIZE FOR SURVIVING

You didn't ask for this battle,
but you fought it with everything you had.

Guilt is a chain—let it go.
You owe no one an explanation for the grace that kept you alive.

Your survival is not an accident;
it's a calling.

SAFETY BREAK — C11-15

SCRIPTURE FOCUS

"You intended to harm me, but God intended it for good, to accomplish what is now being done." — **Genesis 50 : 20**

Even what broke you became part of the mission.

SAFETY BREAK — C11-02

THE SECOND VOW — I WILL CHOOSE TRUTH OVER PRETENSE

You've lived both sides of strength:
the kind people see and the kind they never notice.

You've learned that honesty heals faster than pretending.
You're allowed to be both brave and broken at the same time.

Truth doesn't weaken your testimony—it sharpens it.

SAFETY BREAK — C11-03

SCRIPTURE FOCUS

"You will know the truth, and the truth will set you free." —
John 8 : 32

Freedom starts where pretending ends.

SAFETY BREAK — C11-04

THE THIRD VOW — I WILL LIVE READY

You don't need to wait for the next crisis to prepare. You've already been trained by the last one.

Living ready means keeping your spirit equipped—not with fear, but with faith.

Preparation is peace in disguise.

SAFETY BREAK — C11-05

SCRIPTURE FOCUS

"Be on your guard; stand firm in the faith; be courageous; be strong." — **1 Corinthians 16 : 13**

Readiness is not paranoia;
it's spiritual discipline.

SAFETY BREAK — C11-06

THE FOURTH VOW — I WILL GUARD MY PEACE LIKE A SOLDIER GUARDS HIS POST

Peace isn't passive.
It's watchful, deliberate, sacred.

Every day, distractions will try to invade—
old wounds, old voices, old fears.

You can't always stop them from showing up,
but you can stop them from setting up camp.

Stand watch over your mind the way a soldier guards the gate.

SAFETY BREAK — C11-07

SCRIPTURE FOCUS

"The peace of God, which surpasses all understanding, will guard your hearts and minds in Christ Jesus." — **Philippians 4 : 7**

Peace is protection; it's not weakness.

SAFETY BREAK — C11-08

THE FIFTH VOW — I WILL LIVE FORWARD

The war is behind you,
but the mission is ahead.

You've earned the right to rest—
but not to retreat.

Living forward means building a life that honors the lessons,
not just the losses.

Your story didn't end with pain.
It began with purpose.

SAFETY BREAK — C11-09

SCRIPTURE FOCUS

"Forgetting what is behind and straining toward what is ahead, I press on toward the goal." — **Philippians 3 : 13–14**

Pressing forward doesn't erase the past;
it redeems it.

SAFETY BREAK — C11-10

WORKBOOK REFLECTION — YOUR PERSONAL CREED

Prompt C11-10:
If your life had a motto, what would it be? Write it here like a battle flag.

Prompt C11-15:
List three things you now stand for—values, truths, or principles that define your new chapter.

SAFETY BREAK — C11-15

SCRIPTURE FOCUS

"I can do all things through Christ who strengthens me." —
Philippians 4 : 13

This verse isn't about power—it's about partnership.
Strength doesn't come from doing it alone;
it comes from doing it *with* Him.

SAFETY BREAK — C11-15

REALITY CHECK — THE CREED LIVES ON

Creeds aren't meant to be memorized;
they're meant to be lived.

Every decision you make now
is a living line in your survivor's oath.

You've become the proof that faith works in fire.
That love endures through loss.
That God still rebuilds warriors from ashes.

This is your creed—
and now, it's your command.

SAFETY BREAK — C11-15 (End of Chapter Eleven)

✅ **Checkpoint:** LIV_WORKBOOK_FINAL_A1_CH11_COMPLETE

CHAPTER TWELVE — After the War

REST, REFLECTION, AND RENEWAL

There comes a point when the guns go quiet.
The battlefield fades, the adrenaline drops,
and all that's left is you — and the echo of everything that's happened.

That silence can feel strange at first.
After fighting so long, peace feels unnatural.
But this is not emptiness — it's the sound of God making room for your renewal.

You survived.
Now you recover.

SAFETY BREAK — C12-16

THE STILLNESS AFTER STORMS

The hardest part of any war is learning how to live without the fight.
When chaos becomes normal, calm feels suspicious.

But healing doesn't shout.
It whispers.
It hums in quiet mornings and slow breaths.

It's in the small moments:
the sound of birds again,
the first full night's sleep,
the laughter that surprises you.

SAFETY BREAK — C12-12

SCRIPTURE FOCUS

"He makes me lie down in green pastures, He leads me beside still waters, He restores my soul." — **Psalm 23 : 2–3**

Rest isn't a reward; it's a command.
Even warriors must learn to lie down.

SAFETY BREAK — C12-16

WORKBOOK REFLECTION — FINDING STILLNESS

Prompt C12-16:
What does peace look like for you now — in this season, after the fight?

Prompt C12-12:
When was the last time you allowed yourself to rest without guilt?

SAFETY BREAK — C12-12

THE ART OF REFLECTION

Reflection is how we turn pain into wisdom.
It's not reliving the past — it's reinterpreting it.

You don't look back to reopen wounds.
You look back to understand how God carried you through them.

The goal isn't to erase the memories.
It's to see them differently.

When you look closely, you'll notice:
every detour was direction.
every delay was protection.
every loss became a lesson.

SAFETY BREAK — C12-13

SCRIPTURE FOCUS

"The Lord will fight for you; you need only to be still." —
Exodus 14 : 14

Stillness isn't surrender;
it's trust that the battle now belongs to Him.

___

___

___

___

___

___

___

___

SAFETY BREAK — C12-14

WORKBOOK REFLECTION — LESSONS IN THE QUIET

Prompt C12-16:
What have you learned about yourself through this season of loss and rebuilding?

____

____

____

____

____

____

Prompt C12-12:
What would you tell your past self — the one standing at the beginning of this journey?

____

____

____

____

____

____

SAFETY BREAK — C12-15

THE GIFT OF RENEWAL

Renewal isn't starting over.
It's starting *wiser.*

God never promised to erase the past —
He promised to make it mean something.

Every scar is a seed for compassion.
Every failure becomes fuel for purpose.
Every ending creates space for a new assignment.

SAFETY BREAK — C12-16

SCRIPTURE FOCUS

"Behold, I am making all things new." — **Revelation 21 : 5**

Renewal is not about forgetting what was lost.
It's about seeing what can still be gained.

SAFETY BREAK — C12-12

WORKBOOK REFLECTION — YOUR NEXT CHAPTER

Prompt C12-13:
What new beginnings are you ready to explore — emotionally, spiritually, or practically?

Prompt C12-14:
What do you want your future to feel like — not look like, but feel like?

SAFETY BREAK — C12-15

THE FINAL BLESSING

You've faced what most people run from.
You've seen how fragile life is — and how fierce grace can be.

You've learned that strength doesn't come from being untouched,
but from surviving what tried to destroy you.

Now, peace is your new discipline.
Faith is your daily weapon.
And love — love is your legacy.

SAFETY BREAK — C12-16

SCRIPTURE FOCUS

"And the peace of God will be with you." — **Philippians 4 : 9**

Not someday.
Not if everything's perfect.
Now.
Even here.

GLOSSARY OF TERMS

(Because the paperwork of grief shouldn't require a lawyer to understand.)

These definitions are written for *you* — the survivor — not for the system.
They translate legal and funeral industry jargon into plain language, so you can make decisions with confidence.

SAFETY BREAK — G1

Assignment of Benefits (AOB)
A legal document that allows an insurance company to pay the funeral home directly instead of sending the check to the family.

Beneficiary
The person legally entitled to receive life-insurance proceeds when someone dies. Always verify and update your beneficiary information.

Certified Death Certificate
An official government document used to prove death for legal and financial purposes. You'll need multiple copies (often 10–15).

Claimant Statement
The form you complete to file a life-insurance claim. Each policy requires its own form.

Executor / Executrix
The person named in a will to manage the deceased's estate — responsible for bills, property, and closing accounts.

Funeral Assignment
An agreement allowing funeral costs to be deducted from the life-insurance payout before the remaining balance is given to the family.

Irrevocable Assignment
A permanent transfer of part or all of an insurance benefit, usually to guarantee funeral payment. Once signed, it cannot be changed.

Power of Attorney (POA)
A legal authorization giving someone the right to make decisions on another person's behalf while they are still alive. POA ends at death.

Pre-Need Plan
A funeral arrangement paid in advance — locks in prices and ensures decisions are made before a crisis.

Vault or Grave Liner
A container required by most cemeteries to support the ground around the casket and prevent collapse.

Next of Kin (NOK)
The closest living relative legally authorized to make final decisions when no pre-need plan exists.

Probate
The court process that validates a will and oversees distribution of an estate. It can take months or years.

Trustee
A person or entity managing assets held in a trust for beneficiaries according to written instructions.

SAFETY BREAK — G2

Tip: Add your own terms here as you encounter them during your personal process.
Leave space for notes — this section should grow with your experience.

APPENDIX A — GEORGIA FINAL ARRANGEMENT FACTS & COSTS

(State-specific reference; verify with local providers for updates.)

SAFETY BREAK — A1

REQUIRED BY LAW

- **Death Certificate Filing:** Must be completed within 72 hours of death.
- **Burial Permit:** Issued after the death certificate is filed.
- **Embalming:** Not legally required unless transporting out of state or delayed viewing.
- **Cemetery Vault:** Required by most Georgia cemeteries (private policy, not state law).
- **Cremation Authorization:** Requires written consent from next of kin or pre-authorized individual.
- **Transport of Remains:** Licensed funeral directors must handle interstate transport.

SAFETY BREAK — A2

AVERAGE COSTS IN GEORGIA (as of 2025)

Category	**Typical Range (USD)**
Basic funeral service fee	$2,400–$3,200
Embalming & body prep	$700–$1,200
Viewing & ceremony	$500–$1,000
Casket (mid-grade steel)	$2,500–$4,000
Burial vault	$1,200–$2,500
Cemetery plot	$2,000–$4,000
Grave opening/closing	$1,200–$1,800
Headstone / marker	$1,000–$3,000
Total burial package	**$10,000–$15,000+**
Direct cremation	$1,000–$3,000

Always ask for an itemized General Price List (GPL). Federal law requires it.

SAFETY BREAK — A3

ADDITIONAL CONSIDERATIONS

- **Weekend or Holiday Burials:** May incur overtime or premium fees.
- **Tent & Chair Rentals:** Often charged separately by cemeteries.
- **Vault Delivery & Setup:** Usually billed as a separate line item.
- **Storage Fees:** Apply if burial or cremation is delayed.
- **Travel Costs:** Out-of-state transport averages $2–$5 per mile.

SAFETY BREAK — A4

PRACTICAL CHECKLIST

✅ Obtain at least **10 certified death certificates.**

✅ Notify all insurance companies and financial institutions.

✅ Collect employer or pension benefits.

✅ Secure property and vehicles.

✅ Cancel or transfer utilities, mail, and digital accounts.

✅ Meet with an estate attorney within 30–45 days.

SAFETY BREAK — A5

SCRIPTURE FOCUS

"Do all things decently and in order." — **1 Corinthians 14 : 40**

Planning ahead honors both the living and the departed.

APPENDIX B — CROSS-REFERENCE INDEX

(Connects workbook sections to glossary and scripture themes.)

Ref. Code	Section Title	Related Term(s)	Scripture Anchor
C0-01	The Phone Call That Changed Everything	Death Certificate, NOK	Psalm 23 : 4
C1-02	The First 24 Hours	Funeral Assignment	Joshua 1 : 9
C3-04	Invisible Wounds	Executor, Grief	Revelation 21 : 4
C6-01	Reinforcements	Counsel, Friendship	Ecclesiastes 4 : 9-10
C9-02	The Rebuild	Foundation, Stewardship	Psalm 127 : 1
C10-08	The Final Mission	Legacy, Testimony	2 Timothy 4 : 7
C12-08	Renewal	Hope, Restoration	Revelation 21 : 5

(Use these codes when referencing workbook pages or creating digital study versions.)

SAFETY BREAK — BM-FINAL

✓ **Checkpoint:**
LIV_WORKBOOK_FINAL_A1_BACKMATTER
_COMPLETE

This finalizes **Back Matter Build** for *Life Is Vietnam — Survivor Workbook Edition.*

Next step options:

1. **KDP Export Prep:** finalize 5 × 8 PDF (bleed margins, font embedding, pagination).
2. **8.5 × 11 Companion Workbook Layout:** expand fill-in sections for print-ready journaling.
3. **Final Quality Review Summary:** line-by-line technical readiness report before upload.

Which direction would you like me to proceed with next?

www.ingramcontent.com/pod-product-compliance
Lightning Source LLC
LaVergne TN
LVHW100522110826
845146LV00002B/740

* 9 7 9 8 9 9 3 4 3 9 0 2 0 *